EMPOWERED WOMEN EMPOWER GIRLS

MELODY POURMORADI

ISBN: 978-1-7320980-3-9

ADVANCE PRAISE

"Empowered Women Empower Girls should be mandatory reading for all women. Melody has taken her pain—the pain all women undoubtedly feel growing up in a world where we are obsessively picked apart and held to an impossible standard of perfection—and turned it into her purpose-driven, passionate mission. This guide will inspire you to be your absolute best self, and help you understand the profound ripple effect that comes with that task. Pick this book up now for every woman you know."

-CARA ALWILL, BESTSELLING AUTHOR, HOST OF THE STYLE YOUR MIND PODCAST, AND MINDSET COACH FOR WOMEN ENTREPRENEURS

"In this powerful book, Melody lays down the foundational steps that all women can take to raise up a new generation of heart-centered , empowered women. It starts now, and it starts with us. Whether you are a girl-mom, an entrepreneur or simply a woman looking to uncover her own inner empowerment, allow this book to be your companion and guide. Thank you, Melody, for paving the way for all of us to become the highest versions of ourselves and then shine that light on our future leaders of tomorrow!"

-AMBERLY LAGO, BESTSELLING AUTHOR, HOST OF THE TRUE GRIT AND GRACE PODCAST AND MOTIVATIONAL SPEAKER

"Melody's book Empowered women Empower Girls is just what the doctor ordered! It is a book that is long overdue for the world to read. Every woman was once a girl who had to navigate the ups and downs of life in order to make it to womanhood. That journey is never the same for any two girls. Some have empowered journeys, and some do not, depending on their influences along the way. Melody's book brings to light the tremendous impact an empowered woman can have on the lives of the girls around her. The subconscious and conscious effect we have on girls who are watching us from every corner of the world... especially in our globalized digital social media age. This book is a must-read for every girl and woman in the world. A captivating and riveting read! I believe it will totally transform the way we view our collective responsibility as citizens of this world."

-DR. IYABO WEBZELL, PEDIATRICIAN, AUTHOR, BUSINESS & LIFESTYLE COACH

For you, beautiful reader, for having the courage to look inside yourself and for paving the way for the women of tomorrow.

We have an empowerment gift to share with our community of readers. It can be found at: melodypourmoradi.com/bookbonus

Please join our private Facebook group to connect with other empowered readers! www.facebook.com/groups/empoweredwomenempowergirls

Who would you be today if as a young girl you were taught that you are powerful beyond measure?

CONTENTS

INTRODUCTION

Hello, beautiful readers!

I'm so excited to be taking this journey with you. Thanks for saying YES to yourself {and to our future generation of women}. I bring you this book in partnership with my younger self; a timid, fearful young girl who didn't know her place in the world and dimmed her light at every possible opportunity. Her pain, her insights and her perspective have guided me on my journey of growth and empowerment. As I've evolved into the woman I am today, I have made it my mission to share my tools and my heart with our next generation. You see, I believe at my core that as women, when we have something valuable to share, it is our birthright and our privilege to go out there and deliver our offerings in a way that only we can. My life's work as a coach, girl mom and female empowerment mentor is dedicated to teaching women to get real about their belief systems, access their own superpowers and then share that brilliance with our girls. In fact my entire business can be explained by the title of this book—Empowered Women Empower Girls. This has been my legacy work and as we move deeper into our time together, I will share more about my heart-centered business and mission.

As a side note, I'm thinking that this book could very well have been called Empowered Girls, Empower Women because really, we as women have so much to learn from our young people. I always say this to the women in our GiRLiFE Family—that we must take in the curiosity, fascination and out-of-the-box thinking that is always present in our young girls. These are ways of living that we as women have forgotten and need to re-learn, from our girls. Perhaps this will be the topic of the next book but for now, let's get moving on how we as women can fully show up for ourselves, and in doing so also show up for our girls.

I would like to share with you my definition of certain words so that there's no room for uncertainty.

My definition of empowerment: Being the kindest, most authentic expression of yourself. Knowing who you are, what your gifts are and having the willingness to continue learning and growing each and every day. What takes that empowerment to the next level? Sharing it, in your own unique way.

When I say "our girls" - I am referring to all girls. We all have impressionable young girls in our lives. They may be our daughters, our students or our clients but they are all our girls; a valuable part of the female family. You may believe you are not really of influence to any young girls in particular and this is where I would like to challenge your thinking. As women operating in this world, we are influencing every young girl we come into contact with in some way, and most of the time we don't even notice it. These young girls are watching us, hearing us and picking up on our cues of what it is to be a woman. Never underestimate the power of your presence and your influence. You've got some brilliant young minds following your lead. By accessing empowerment in your own life, you will be modeling for our girls how to move through every moment as a powerful, lit up woman. Once we can truly comprehend and access the influence of our personal power, together we will do the collective "heart work" necessary to show our girls how it's done!

I also want to acknowledge that while parts of this book may resonate most with women who were conditioned as women in society from the time they were young, it is a book for all women—that includes anyone who identifies as a woman at any point in their lives. We are all shaping the future by being our most authentic selves.

HOW TO MOVE THROUGH THIS BOOK

At the start of each chapter in this book, I'll share a personal quote that outlines how we as women can evolve and uplevel ourselves. Next, I'll explain how we can deliver this empowerment straight to our girls. Most of the time it doesn't actually involve doing or saying anything new to our girls, but rather just being different. That's where the true POWER in empowerment comes in—when we lead by example. At the end of each chapter, I will propose a few different exercises to get you reflecting on each chapter because unless we commit to practicing new ways of thinking and being, nothing really changes. To get the most out of this book, I strongly encourage you to use the prompts I give you and honestly answer the questions. During our time together, we will call them our heart-work. Following the heart-work, I've also included a few empty reflection pages at the end of each chapter. Feel free to use these pages for additional notes, drawings, or reflections as you move along. I promise your personal reflections are where the magic happens.

While the name of the book states that empowered women can empower girls, the truth is that we can never really give empowerment to anyone. They need to want it for themselves. That's why it's so important for me to share and share again throughout this book that when we become the most authentic, powerful expression of ourselves, our girls will follow our lead, they will see how it's done, and they will embody that empowerment because it's what they are seeing and experiencing, in us. It's all about modeling and being the change we wish to see in them.

Does reading this book and claiming your own empowerment give you a surefire guarantee that the young girl in your life is going to be a powerhouse and succeed at everything she does? Mmmm, that's a solid no. I can promise you this though… She will be in a much better position to claim her own inner light by watching you embody the highest and greatest expression of yourself. So while I know you picked up this book to empower the special girls in your life, moving forward, I want you to make your primary goal to empower YOURself. I know that seems counterintuitive, but I promise this book will guide you, and by the end, it will make more sense.

Please respect this space we are creating together as a judgment-free zone. That means that while you are moving through the pages of this book, especially while you are thinking about and answering your heart-work prompts, be kind to yourself. Do not judge what comes up. Sit with it and know that if it's coming through you, it's meant to be part of your journey through this work. As we move through our time here together, I will challenge you and nudge you in some new and potentially uncomfortable ways. I will invite you to change perceptions that you've held for most of your life. Do I have your permission to do that?

As a final note, I invite you to bring your younger self along with you as you make your way through this book. As you gain new insights and uncover new ways of claiming your empowered life, I want her to do the same. So keep her in your heart and try to stay connected to what her thoughts, fears, challenges and desires were as she was growing up. That eight year old version of you is cheering the hardest for you. She wants you to win. She will hold the space, but you've got to make the moves.

Buckle up, beauties. We are about to go on an illuminating ride together. I invite you to start reading with a genuine willingness to change the belief systems that no longer work for you. That will be our starting point to create new, more encouraging thought patterns for ourselves and our future generation of women. As Maya Angelou said, "Do the best you can until you know better. Then when you know better, do better." Let's do better together.

Below, I'm leaving some space for you to share what your intentions are for reading this book. I know there's a reason you picked it up and are putting aside the time and energy to dive in. It will help to get clear on what you hope to get out of our time together so that as you're reading, you can check in with yourself to make sure your learning is in alignment with your intentions.

My intentions for reading this book include:

____

____

____

____

Thanks for saying yes to yourself!

Happy reading, lovely.

XOXO,
Melody

CHAPTER 1
I AM NOT A PERFECT WOMAN

"There is no virtue in the quest for perfection. Trying to create perfection will rob you of expressing and experiencing anything meaningful in your life."

I am not a perfect woman.

I feel a strong pull to share this with you right at the beginning of our journey together. If you were hoping to read a book written by a perfect woman, you've come to the wrong place. I'm most definitely not your girl, and I most certainly never will be.

I am fallible. I make mistakes. I fall off course. I lose sight of what's important. I let my emotions get the better of me. I judge myself. I highlight my weaknesses. I fail to celebrate my victories. I don't always know the right thing to say. I experience anxiety daily.

I stumble more often than not through my own challenges and rites of passage, but I always remember where my power lies and choose new responses, new thoughts, and new actions when I notice that misalignment within me. Isn't that the best that any of us can do? As I fall, grow and evolve through my various roles in life, I share what I learn because, after all, isn't that what sisterhood is about—sharing our pain and growth so we can be better as a collective?

In an honest effort to keep it real for you, I feel the need to share my "imperfections." Not too long ago, I was on a quest to be the most perfect version of myself, but the exact opposite holds true for me today. My greatest goal today is to show up as me….raw and real. And isn't that the most profound offering anyone can share— their truth?

I'm sure there have been moments where you got a peak into another woman's life and you were certain that she had it all figured out and that her world was the epitome of sheer perfection. It wasn't. I know that deep within, you already know that.

I recently had a conversation with one of my childhood best friends where I was venting to her about some deep and difficult stuff that was going on in my life as a result of my ongoing challenge with anxiety. She responded in shock, still after more than 35 years of knowing me, not able to understand how the way I come across to people is so different from the way I feel at times. And it felt cathartic for me to be witnessed in this state of vulnerability. Conversations like this remind me that it's so important to share what's challenging us, especially with the women around us. We get this beautiful opportunity to let them know that they are not alone. To make them feel seen, heard and witnessed. I'm committing to having more conversations like this in hopes that we can remove the stigma associated with not having it all together all of the time. Instead, I want us to rock what we've got, especially when it's not neat and tidy, the way we are conditioned to believe women must present themselves to be.

So while I'm not perfect, I am committed to my evolution. I am committed to being better and bolder every day and, when I have a weak moment, I do my best to give myself some grace and choose again.

If I were attached to being perfect, I wouldn't be writing this book for fear of how it might be received. I wouldn't have created a girls empowerment business without a guaranteed certainty that it would have the impact I so wished to bring forth. I would still be wishing and waiting for the conditions to be optimal and I would never have made the moves necessary to get this movement off the ground. The GiRLiFE program to date has introduced thousands of girls across the globe to their superpowers. Imagine if I hadn't stepped out of my own fears of imperfection to start this mission—so many girls would have been missing the inner tools that our facilitators deliver to them. I share this not to boast but rather to share that everything I've been able to accomplish up until this point is the honest effort of a very imperfect woman.

Despite the moves I've made toward my mission, I continue to have moments on my journey to and through confidence, courage and self-love where I doubt myself. I have many moments where I ask, "Who am I to be writing a book on empowerment?" Other moments, I wonder how this world of self-reflection has become so deeply ingrained in my being. In writing this book, it was paramount for me to explore these thoughts and questions so that I could be straight with myself and be completely straight with you. I am and always have been on a quest to understand and evolve myself since I was a young girl. I didn't know it then, but I was obsessed with finding a way to feel comfortable in my own skin. I was seeking my place in the world, and I was looking to find my own power, whatever it may have looked like for me at the time. While I am still doing those things today, I am doing them with a little more experience, research and understanding under my belt.

The more I got through writing the chapters of this book and re-reading them, the more the answers I so needed were revealed to me. So I came back to this section, beautiful reader, to properly introduce the book that I've written for you: the book I have written for us. Empowerment is my message to share because of my deep commitment to continually find it within myself. Empowerment is my gift to give because the ongoing journey to finding it is the greatest gift I ever could have given myself.

The way I see it, it's always better to create that impact by taking imperfect action than by never doing the thing and wondering what if. Not to mention all of the ways you would be withholding from yourself and the world the many gifts you have to share, just because you were waiting and wishing.

You will hear me talking A LOT in this book about perfection and how we must find a way to stop seeing any virtue in trying to attain it. I believe that there is a perfection epidemic, and I will share as much as I need to on this topic to help combat this way of thinking that is robbing us all from reaching our greatest potential.

Perfection will never come. But you—real, raw and willing to take a deep dive into your own empowerment? That's where the gold is, and I can't think of a better way to set our girls up for their own empowerment journey.

Do yourself a favor and don't make perfection part of the plan because when you do, you hinder your ability to be in a state of joy and peace while navigating this forever-changing thing we call life.

Screw perfection… Let's go!

HEART ♥ WORK

What would you do if you didn't have to be perfect?

Who would you be if you didn't have to be perfect?

REFLLECTIONS

REFLECTIONS

CHAPTER 2
YOU ARE POWERFUL BEYOND MEASURE

"You are powerful beyond measure."

These are the first words we share with every young girl who walks into any of our workshops. It doesn't matter where in the world she lives and what her experiences have been up until now. What matters is that she knows as early as humanly possible that she is brilliant beyond measure and that she is a powerful creator in her own life. This is how we set our girls up for success, on their terms

Was this a message that was shared with you when you were a young girl?

Me neither.

I was told a lot of things, but not this. This kind of ideology simply was not customary for girls to be taught, at least not while I was growing up. Even the most mindful parents among us weren't speaking like this because messaging like this was not part of anyone's narrative at the time.

We were taught to be good.

We were taught to be pretty.

We were taught to behave like good girls do.

We were taught to care about what "they" will think. (Who are "they" anyway?)

We were taught to respect our elders, even when our elders sucked.

You know the drill.

What we weren't taught is that there is a power source inside each of us that once activated, could impact our entire lives for the better.

Now, I want to share all of this with the caveat that our parents and the elders in our lives who conveyed this messaging to us were doing the best they could with the knowledge and information they had available to them at the time. Truth is, they were just teaching us what they were taught. As children, we accept the words and perceptions of our elders as the truth. We love them and we trust them and that's good enough for us as little kids. More on this later.

THE ONLY PERSON YOU HAVE POWER OVER IS YOU

I know that at times we wish we had power over someone else. We wish we could will someone to do better or feel better or be better, but that's just not how it goes. While we have influence over how some things will play out in our own lives, we don't get to directly control another person's actions or behaviors. So that piece about us being powerful beyond measure? That only ever applies to you, and trying to change someone else will never work, so let's not even try. Keep your focus on the only person who you can help transform: YOU. People may behave differently or make different choices because they've been in your presence and they've experienced that empowered energy firsthand, but that's not because you set out to change them. It's because they were ready for change and your embodiment of it inspired them. Insightful stuff, eh?

LOOK INSIDE

Everything you need, want and desire must first be found on the inside. Did you hear me, beautiful reader? Perhaps one of the most important things I want to share with you is that all that you seek outside of yourself, in your relationships, in your work, in your spiritual practice, etc. must first be located inside of you. We can't wish and wait for someone or something outside of us to provide us with that which we haven't yet been able to provide for ourselves. Love, loyalty, friendship, kindness… they all are an inside job at first. I dare you to try to find something of value that you don't have to first locate within. Just try. So when we step into feelings of unworthiness or lack, we must ask ourselves, "What do I need right now, and how can I provide that thing for myself?" Want a loving partner? Re-examine how loving you have been with yourself and course correct. Looking for respect from someone you admire? How are you respecting yourself in this moment? Want to feel worthy? Notice your own relationship with worthiness. It all starts on the inside.

HOW DOES THIS APPLY TO OUR GIRLS?

It's simple, really… If we want our next generation of girls to fully own and harness their power, we must teach them to take responsibility for themselves. Once they really understand this, they can choose with intention and they can start activating that power in every area of their lives. The first step is simply knowing that it exists. Our job is to role model that inner power. I often allow my girls to witness my inner self-talk. I purposely walk them through my thought process of how I move from a challenge to a choice. I want them to see how I map out the path from feeling powerless in a situation to reclaiming my power over a given scenario. Sometimes, the highest form of empowerment is simply surrendering to the fact that over certain situations, we actually have no power. Either way, I love showing them that while I most certainly don't have all the answers, I can use my inner tools at all times and access my personal power to navigate life. P.S. - The scenario I just described can only be accessed when I am feeling truly connected to myself. Believe me, there are days when I'm a hot mess, and modeling for my girls is not my first go-to. We're all human, and, in every moment, we need to at least try to access the most empowered version of ourselves. When we can't, we can take a deep breath, forgive ourselves and recalibrate.

Everything is a choice. How you show up for these messages, what you allow into your life and what you release… it's ALL a choice.

ONE LAST THING ON POWER…

Finding and plugging into our power source is unique in every moment. There will be days when our power will come from taking a three-mile run and feeling strong and rooted in our foundation. There will be other days when our power will come from having a good cry so that we can feel what we need to feel, without judging ourselves for it. Whatever the situation may be, our power comes from getting in tune with what we need, when we need it, and finding our own way to be the deliverer of that need.

HEART ❤ WORK

What are some beliefs you were taught as a young girl that you choose to release?

What are some new belief systems that you would like to adopt moving forward?

REFLECTIONS

REFLECTIONS

CHAPTER 3
HOW WE RESIST EMPOWERMENT

"It is only when we start becoming conscious of how we block our own empowerment that we can start stepping into the most powerful expression of ourselves."

In order to truly step into our empowerment, we must acknowledge how much we've blocked it from flowing into our lives until now. I know what you're thinking—"Why on earth would I block something so freaking impactful from entering my life?" Here's the thing. So often we resist things subconsciously because of programming that we received as young girls. Since 95% of our brain is our subconscious mind, more often than we realize, we are acting out scripts and stories that we're not even aware exist. Now that you're tuned into this idea, you can become more mindful of how the old stuff might be playing out in your life (up until now). You will also tune into how you can make a shift that will prime you for the empowerment you so deeply crave for yourself and for our girls. So let's do this—let's bring our awareness to all the ways we've unknowingly participated in our own disempowerment and perhaps, continue to do so. I realize the ideas I'm proposing might seem benign, but I encourage you to read on with an open heart. Trust that getting curious about some of these factors might give you the direct edge you are seeking to expand your own empowerment game.

PARTICIPATING IN GOSSIP

Talking behind another woman's back in anything but a positive way is gossip. Notice the times when you are having conversations that veer toward finding fault in other women and in some way making them wrong… They're too this or they're too that. We all get sucked into this negative web of shit talk, and as a woman seeking empowerment in this space, this is your gentle reminder that this kind of dialogue needs to stop. Speaking ill of other women is nothing but a reflection of our own insecurities. It's an unevolved way of bringing someone else down in hopes that it may raise us up in some way. It doesn't. It only keeps us stuck and small. So the next time you notice yourself falling into those old patterns, consider asking yourself, how can I vocalize something kind about the woman being talked about instead? If you've got nothing kind to say (it happens), find a way to change the topic of conversation. I always say to my girls, "Don't talk behind someone's back unless you're speaking of them with kindness and good intent." That being said, I am boldly aware of the moments of weakness where I too fall into this old pattern and remind myself that it's not necessarily about what I say to them but it's more about what I model for them. Once your circle takes note of the fact that you're no longer available for that kind of "bonding," they will stop sharing their unfriendly chatter with you. It's actually a worthy opportunity for all of you to bring more intention to the kinds of conversations you hold space for when you hang out together.

COMPETING WITH OTHER WOMEN

Sadly and to our own detriment, there are still women who compete, undermine and degrade one another. How can we expect to stop being oppressed by men when there are women still oppressing one another? Understand that there is no competition here whatsoever. The beauty and brilliance that we witness in other women is only a reflection and a reminder of the light that exists within all of us. The next time you find yourself experiencing feelings of envy or wishing that you could achieve what another woman else already has, allow it to be a source of inspiration for you to know and believe that the possibilities for you too are endless.

I used to get painfully envious of other women. I would see their accomplishments and chosen circumstances and I would feel so down on myself that I couldn't be and achieve those things. It wasn't until I changed my belief system around envy that I could step into a new way of operating in the world. My core thoughts changed because, after all, a belief is a thought that we keep thinking. I started seeing other women as my inspiration. I saw them as proof that success could be had by all of us. I stopped seeing myself as separate from them and started viewing us as a collective. I started searching for ways that

I could learn from them. This mindset shift changed everything for me. Today, running a business that is all about female empowerment, I see women as my partners-in-shine: a term that we use on the regular in my business. Together, we are co-creators bringing light to ourselves, to one another and to the girls we serve. What a gift I was able to give myself by putting aside feelings of envy and allowing that sistering and collaborative energy to flow in. Let's lift each other up, beautiful women! That's where our power source is—in our collaboration, not in our competition.

MAKING SOMEONE ELSE'S OPINION OF OURSELVES MORE IMPORTANT THAN OUR OWN OPINION OF OURSELVES

If I asked you how often you think twice about doing something for fear of someone else's thoughts, opinions and judgments of it, what would your honest answer be? I totally feel you if you answered, "All the time!" We are trained as young girls to be super conscious about how others perceive us. We're told to be good girls and the way we interpret what it means to be "good" is so subjective and often burdensome. We set ourselves on fire to keep others warm, paying no attention to our own needs, wants and self-perceptions. No doubt that in some way, you have put aside your own goals, ambitions and voice because you thought it wouldn't be enough for some people or too much for others. This ends now. You, beautiful reader, must flex that self-love muscle in moments like these and tune out the voices that stop you from being, creating, enjoying and truly living. You get one life, and the last thing I want for you is to have regrets when the possibilities of today are no longer available to you in the same way down the road. Turn up the volume on your own inner magic. Those who can't handle it will naturally filter themselves out of your daily life, and those who love it will show up for more of it. Either way, you keeping it real is attracting more that is aligned with YOU into your life.

GIVING AWAY OUR POWER

Too often, we play the blame game. This one's a biggie. We find ourselves in a negative situation, and we immediately look outside ourselves to see what role a circumstance or another person may have played in making that happen. We were never really taught to look inside and ask ourselves, What role did I play in bringing this situation into my life? Now I'm not saying we need to self-sabotage by being hard on ourselves for every single thing because, yes, some things do happen that are out of our control. I'm simply suggesting that we often forget what powerful creators we are in our own lives on a moment-to-moment basis. It is important to be open to the ways in which our thought patterns, actions and behaviors call certain things into our lives. When we blame, we literally give our power away. Why? Because we are affirming that the solution to the problem at hand is outside of us instead of inside. When we have to seek a resolution to a situation on the outside, we give up our ability to be an active participant in creating a solution. Is this making sense? Let me give you an example. I used to struggle a lot with creating meaningful friendships from the time I was growing up and then well into adulthood. I was always questioning why I had friends who didn't have my best interest at heart or didn't care much about what was going on in my life. I believed it what a crazy coincidence that the same type of people would always become my "best friends." And truthfully, I was getting annoyed because, after all, a best friend should think and ask about you, right? I was developing anger about the situation and even more anger toward my so-called friends. This went on for years before I realized that this was all a result of the types of people I was attracting. I noticed that in my friendships, I wasn't volunteering any information about my own life. I was always the one asking the questions, playing the supporting role and taking a back seat to my own life. Somehow I believed that whatever my friends were dealing with was way more important than anything I may have been dealing with. A deep, long look in the mirror and some serious reflection taught me that if I wanted to bring more two-way, mutually beneficial friendships into my life, I would need to start advocating for myself and actually becoming a part of the relationship rather than playing the cheerleader role all the time. Had I not looked within to understand how I had a hand in creating this scenario, I would still be having the same experience.

BELIEVING IN MESSAGES THAT DISEMPOWER WOMEN

There are so many low-vibe narratives floating around about women, and often we passively accept them as truth without questioning their validity:

- "Be sure to marry rich."

- "Women are too emotional."
- "If you're too smart or strong, you won't find a man."
- "Girls are dramatic by nature."
- "If a boy is mean to you, that means he likes you."
- "She must be acting up because it's her time of month.
- "You would be so pretty if you wore some makeup."

We must question these statements before we take them on as truth. Sometimes we women have gotten so used to this type of banter that we don't even notice or question it. This has got to change. We get to decide what stays and what goes simply by eliminating certain words and phrases from our own daily narrative.

FEARING SUCCESS

Often, we block our own empowerment because we feel scared of the potential success that may come our way. Yes, you heard me correctly. We fear change, we fear growth, we fear judgment. But most of the time, we fear our own light. We fear what is on the other side of the success that we so deeply seek. We don't want anything to disrupt our "comfort." Here's the thing, though—true empowerment can only be reached when we find the courage to take a small step out of that highly coveted comfort zone. There's so much magic in taking a shot on what's on your heart. When we make a decision to become an energetic match for our desires, we are sending a signal to the universe to start co-creating with us. So what's it going to be, beautiful reader? Will you stop blocking your own success? When I notice myself pushing against opportunities because I've hit my own self-imposed upper limit, I ask myself, Melody, how good can you handle it? This is a reminder to me that it's my ultimate success I'm fearing and not my fear of failure. Your hiding is not actually serving anyone. It's time to step up and step in.

NOT ACCEPTING A COMPLIMENT

Can you take a compliment? No, really. Let's be honest for a moment. When another human shares that they are witnessing a positive attribute in you, do you graciously accept it, or do you find a way to deflect it? I was recently having lunch with a dear friend who I hadn't seen in a while. As we sat down, I took notice of how radiant she looked, and I let her know. When I am making a positive observation about someone, I always make a point to share it with them because I know that, as women, we absolutely need to do more of that. What came next? My friend started reciting a list of all the reasons that she didn't actually look good. It was all the products she was using, or a new shade of hair color that she had recently switched to that contributed to what I was seeing in her. When I gently pointed out to her what she was doing, she continued on, and insisted that it was her new lash serum or the bronzer that she had recently purchased. Her soliloquy was just another example of how, as women, we sometimes deflect positivity as it's coming our way.

THE WAY WE GREET A GIRL FOR THE FIRST TIME

When you are speaking with a girl or you meet a young girl for the first time… how do you greet her? When I was growing up, I noticed this all around me; well-meaning adults saying hello to a young girl, and the first thing that would pop out of their mouths would be, "You're so pretty" or "How cute are you?" I am for sure guilty of this myself. It seems natural to say something that you yourself have heard others say a million times. But we really need to check ourselves and become aware of how our words and actions may be shaping the young girls in our lives. Consistently focusing on a girl's outer appearance instead of her inner intelligence can be SO detrimental. Making her looks a primary focus encourages her to form unhealthy and unreasonable expectations of herself. It invites her to put all of her energy into improving her outer beauty rather than expanding her mind. Alternative ways of acknowledging a young girl could be by saying, "You're so strong," "You're so brilliant," or "You're so kind," You could also ask them a question like, "What's new and good?" or "Have you read any cool books lately?" There are so many thought-provoking questions you could ask that would set you both up for an inspiring and intelligent conversation. If you do want to compliment her outer appearance, find ways to highlight her natural beauty as it relates to her whole self so that you are not necessarily focusing on the features, but rather on the person who possesses them. An example could be, "I love the way your face lights up when you're doing something you enjoy."

Unfortunately, the list of how we disempower ourselves goes on and on but my hope is that now that you're tuned into how often we women do this, you will start to course correct. I want you to start catching yourself in the moments where you are actually pushing that empowerment away and then gently choosing again.

HEART ❤ WORK

How have you resisted your own empowerment until now?

What are some new ways that you are now willing to step into your empowerment?

REFLECTIONS

REFLECTIONS

CHAPTER 4
GOOD GIRL NO MORE

"Sometimes we need to unlearn what we've been taught in order to re-learn a newer, more empowering way of operating in the world."

The first thing I would love to see you do is to release some of the messaging you received as a young girl. I hope that's cool with you. It's an important first step to clear out and set yourself up for success.

We are groomed as young girls to be super conscious about how others perceive us. We're told to be "good girls" and our interpretation of that request is so subjective and so unbelievably heavy. I want you to think back on how many times you were told as a young girl to be "good."

I polled our Facebook community about what they felt was being asked of them when they were told to be "good," and these are the answers they came up with:

- Follow the rules.

- Agree with your elders.
- Don't cause conflict.
- Mask how you truly feel.
- Don't challenge other people's ideas.
- Don't disagree with anyone.
- Be likeable.
- Be polite at ALL costs.
- Be seen, not heard.
- Be ladylike.
- Be quiet.
- Don't speak until spoken to.

In essence, we were being told:

- to be what we are not
- to make others feel good even when we are NOT feeling good
- that what other people want and need from us is more important than what we want and need for ourselves
- to follow the rules at all costs (are boys taught to follow the rules?)

So, we put on mask upon mask upon mask and we wonder, as grown women, why it's been so hard to live a life that is true to who we are. At this point, we're not even sure who we are. We've heard this request so many times that we don't question it anymore. It's so ingrained that many of us make the same requests of our girls to be "good."

This is so damaging to us as girls and so damaging to us as women…

Let's take this a step further. If being a good girl is defined by the points mentioned, then wouldn't the following list of traits be associated with being "bad"?

Someone who:

- breaks the rules
- challenges other people's ideas
- says how she feels
- speaks her truth even when others disagree
- makes her voice heard
- keeps it real
- is true to herself
- makes her presence known
- takes up space

Now, I don't know about you, but the points I just listed above are my greatest wish for every woman and girl. I'm going to propose that we stop asking our girls to be "good" and teach them instead to be powerful.

How does that feel for you?

Are you still with me?

If so, how can we teach girls to be powerful?

I think it's a lot simpler than we realize. Here are a couple of ideas to start with.

TEACH THEM ABOUT THEIR INTUITION

One of the most impactful lessons we like to share in our empowerment groups is the importance of trusting our own intuition. We teach our girls that intuition is "the voice of your heart" or "that deep inner voice of knowing." Some refer to it as that gut feeling that tries to signal things to us on the regular. As I mentioned above, by asking girls to be "good," we are in essence teaching them to turn outwards for guidance. Our goal is to get girls to tune inward for answers instead—that's their most trusted GPS, and it will lead them in the direction of their highest good.

Trusting our intuition = Trusting ourselves.

We want to give girls messaging that gets them more connected with their inner voice of knowing, not messaging that blocks them from communicating with it. A simple example is this: When the young girl in your life comes to you asking what she should do about a challenge she is experiencing, instead of jumping in and giving her all the "right" answers, (which are answers that are unique to only you, by the way), ask her this simple question:

"What is your intuition telling you to do?"

I can't tell you how many times I've asked this question of my daughters and the girls in our workshops. The answers they come up with are everything! The truth is, they already know what the next right action step is. They're just not used to flexing that intuitive muscle that is available to them at all times, in all places, for all things. It's another power source within, and igniting it will set them up to be unstoppable. We get to help them access that empowerment by simply asking questions that remind them how powerful they are instead of stepping in and taking over, which tends to be our natural go-to.

TEACH GIRLS THAT MANY ANSWERS THEY SEEK ARE ALREADY INSIDE OF THEM

Everything you need is already within you. Do you believe me when I say this?

We all do this: when we're faced with a problem or need a quick hit of advice, we proceed to ask anyone who will listen how to handle it… our sister, mother, BFF, the list goes on for sure. Why don't we ask ourselves? Who knows more about our life, our experiences, our thoughts and our wishes than we do? To be a powerful woman, we MUST become our own most trusted resource and confidante. We must start knowing and believing that, first and foremost, most of the questions we need answers to are on the inside. How powerful is that? How powerful are you? Very powerful. It's never too late to adopt these perspectives. This, beautiful reader, is your invitation to step into your most powerful self.

HEART ❤ WORK

What would your life look like if, as a young girl, you were taught to be a "powerful girl"?

Who would you be today if you weren't constantly concerned with upsetting others?

What could you have created if you didn't wait for that permission slip you've been waiting on?

How often do you tune into what your intuition is trying to tell you?

REFLECTIONS

REFLECTIONS

CHAPTER 5
I'M A MODEL… YOU KNOW WHAT I MEAN?

"Our girls are watching us and they're hearing us. They're picking up on our cues of how to love themselves. Find every opportunity to be gentle, respectful and loving to yourself."

Beautiful women of the world, you are all models. You are all examples to our next generation of what it is to be a woman. Your thoughts, your behaviors and your unique gifts are shaping our girls.

I distinctly remember being a child and witnessing the women around me. In every moment, I was drawing my own conclusions about what it really means to be a woman. With every interaction, I was taking notes and writing the script of my own life… and I am certain these female influencers were not aware of my impressionable eyes on them.

There was a subconscious dialogue going on in my head—one that I was not aware of at the time but, looking back, it's all so clear to me. As a grown woman, it's been very insightful for me to take a good long look at myself and re-examine my belief systems. How were they shaped by the experiences of the women around me? And how have my belief systems influenced the way I view the world?

I was left with a tapestry of questions each time I interacted with the different women who entered my world.

What did they bring out in me?

Did they like me?

Did I like them?

How were they perceived by the people around them?

Were they an example of who I want to be?

Were they the exact example of who I don't want to be?

I ALWAYS FEEL LIKE SOMEBODY'S WATCHING ME...

Live life as an example. We have some very impressionable young minds following our lead. As I talked about earlier, as young girls, we subconsciously picked up on the cues of the women in our lives. We looked up to them because they were older, and we were taught to listen to and respect our elders. So much so that we started to emulate them. For some girls, this was an incredible blessing because the women who led them were self-aware, overall positive people. For other girls, however, they were following the lead of women who were just trying their best to make it through the day themselves. These women didn't have access to their inner tools, let alone having the mindset to nurture the next generation with intention. They were doing the best they could with the limited resources they had available to them.

NO HARD FEELINGS

If you were in the latter group, where the women in your life were examples you didn't respect or want to emulate, it's totally okay. They were doing the best they could with their particular set of life circumstances. When we choose to see it that way, we're better able to forgive them and choose a different way for ourselves. Isn't that why we're here together after all, doing this work of unlearning and relearning? We're here because we want to be a part of the change. We want to choose a more empowering intergenerational narrative. Every relationship is a spiritual assignment, and if we're willing to do the homework, there's a lot we can learn about how we want to operate (and how we wish NOT to operate) in the world. Forgiveness and release will actually be your greatest allies in feeling the peace that you wish to pay forward. Holding onto past resentments will only have you tuned into a life where you attract more to be upset and annoyed with on the regular. Let it go, lovely. It's not serving you to stay in a state of resentment over something that happened in the past. That's never where your power is. Your power is, and always will be, in the present moment. So please, don't go giving it away so easily.

MAKE SELF-LOVE A PRIORITY

Bring to mind a girl in your life and understand that she will follow your lead when it comes to self-image and body image. Witnessing that you have a positive relationship with yourself will impact her relationship with herself in so many significant ways. Give her as many opportunities as possible to see you speak to yourself with self-respect and self-love. Realize that the words you use are paramount in setting the stage for her own inner dialogue. Sometimes we say things out loud that are highlighting our weaknesses. If we're being honest, we do this pretty often... more often than we realize. I will always remember an experience I had with my daughter while we were in a fitting room together trying clothes on. She couldn't have been more than 8 or 9 years old at the time. We were hearing the disparaging dialogue that two friends were having in the fitting room next to us. They were each talking about their various body parts being too big, too this, too that, not enough this, not enough that… you know what I'm talking about. I will never forget the look on my daughter's face as she heard the women speaking this way to each other about themselves. I knew that we would be having a deeply intense conversation about it on the car ride home. My daughter's exact words were, "Mommy, why are they being so mean to themselves?" It broke my heart to hear her say this because I knew that that conversation would be filed away somewhere deep in her subconscious mind and may come up when she is staring at her own reflection in the mirror at some point not too far into the future. It also made me feel for the two women who were being so painfully harsh on themselves. No doubt that they too had heard women speaking in this way to themselves when they were growing up. What did I share at the beginning of this book? That as women walking this earth, we are ALL influencers in the lives of every young girl we come into contact with. This example is all the proof I needed to believe it at my core. Truth is, women are not born hating themselves. We live in a society that teaches us to scrutinize our every move as women. We live in a society that actually profits from our self-doubt. We live in a society that needs some change, and WE are the women who are going to deliver that change to our next generation. How are we going to take that lead? By becoming our own greatest supporter, first and foremost.

SUPPORT OTHER WOMEN

This point right here is non-negotiable. Women supporting women is everything when it comes to modeling true heart-centered lead(her)ship for our girls. One of the greatest privileges of my life is that I get to support and be supported by other women. It's worth mentioning once more that, as women, we get to hold mirrors up to one another that encourage us to truly see ourselves and evolve. We get to reflect back to one another what is possible for all of us. Another woman's victory is yours to be celebrated. How beautiful it is to celebrate her wins without questioning your own worth? And when you're winning, turn around and help another woman because you remember how sacred it felt to be held by the women who came before you. How fortunate we are to all be in this together.

STOP SENDING MIXED SIGNALS

Remember, claiming your own empowerment is the greatest gift you can give to our next generation. To make this a true priority, we must be kind, gentle and loving with ourselves first. It's not okay to be unkind to yourself and then to be disappointed when you see the young girl in your life mistreating herself. That kind of messaging will only set her up for confusion. Know that she is picking up on ALL of your habits: what you eat, how you speak, etc. Even the type of people you choose to surround yourself with will impact her immediate circle of friends. Check in with yourself as often as possible to make sure that you are sending our impressionable young girls the most empowering messaging. When I look at my daughters, I can so clearly see in the everyday moments how my relationship with myself has made an impression on them. I can see how some of the ways I love and honor myself have taken form in their own lives, and I can also see how some of my fears and challenges have become their fears and challenges too. This is an absolute reminder to me that the work I do on myself is paramount, not just for me, but for them too. As Naomi Wolf says, ""A Mother who radiates self-love and self-acceptance actually vaccinates her daughter against low self-esteem.". Let's ALL vaccinate OUR daughters, OUR girls, against low self-esteem and witness the beautiful shifts and transformations that come about as a result for all of us. You deserve to take every opportunity to show yourself how worthy you truly are.

Can I make a request? From here on out, whether you are looking in the mirror with pride or simply accepting a compliment with grace, BE respectful to yourself. When you catch yourself in a familiar pattern of negative self-talk, whether or not the girls you're influencing are present, make a conscious decision to create a new, more empowering message to yourself. You always have the power to choose again, and it's never too late to create a new positive pattern. I PROMISE YOU that whether your girl acknowledges it or not, she will take notice and internalize the positive shifts in you and use them as a cue to love and respect herself more.

HEART ❤ WORK

What are some behaviors you have unknowingly modeled that you DON'T want to pass down to our next generation?

What are some new empowering behaviors you would like to take on for yourself?

REFLECTIONS

REFLECTIONS

CHAPTER 6
WATCH THAT LANGUAGE

"My words create my world. The words I speak today are creating my reality for tomorrow and every day after that."

OUR LANGUAGE CREATES OUR REALITY

Did you know that we can actually speak things into (and out of) existence?

Sometimes we can even convince ourselves of things that aren't true because we've given the words we're speaking so much energy that they actually start becoming our experience in the world. Of course, as with all things, this can work for us or against us depending on what direction we choose to aim that influence in. Yes, we are such powerful creators, yet more often than not we don't even realize the magnitude of that power. Not only can our language keep us feeling in a low, uncomfortable vibe, but what we rarely realize is how our words introduce who we are to the people around us. So when we constantly speak in a negative, low-vibe way people feel that quite quickly and don't want to be around us.

Have you ever noticed yourself literally clam up in the presence of people who spew their negative narratives everywhere they go?

I know when I first tuned into this idea, it changed my interactions with others in such an impactful way. In some cases, I noticed the power I had to attract the right people into my world through my choice of language. This is exactly what's helped me create an inner circle of women I'm proud to call my friends and colleagues. In other cases, I was so uncomfortable with the language being used around me that I had to adjust how much space I was holding for negative people in my life. Nobody wants to hang out with a negative Nelly and if they do, or if you do, maybe it's time to start making some changes around the vibe you're creating space for in your life.

When we're young, let's say before the age of 9 because statistically that's the age when a girl's self-confidence peaks, we are living in a state of possibility. Our words are creating a bright and a beautiful reality. We're curious, hopeful and so present. We were never concerned with what others thought of us. We just were, and we reflected that in the stories we told and the interactions that we had.

I'm going to share some of the words and inner dialogue that I was speaking out as a child.

These were some of the things I was saying and feeling before age 9:

"I'm perfect as I am."

"There's nothing I can't do!"

"There's always a way!"

"I love myself!"

"I've got this!"

Life was a beautiful declaration back then. In essence, a statement—one that didn't need anyone else's backing because it was so rooted in my own certainty. While I can't speak for every young girl, after 14 years of working with women and girls, I can say with a great deal of conviction that I was not alone in these sentiments.

I then reflect back on some of my inner dialogue from when I was in my teenage years. My language towards myself became much harsher. I was my own worst critic. I stopped making statements and started asking questions about what the world wanted from me. I couldn't stand the sight of my own reflection in the mirror. It hurts me so deeply to have to write these words for you, but I'm keeping it real here, knowing that if I felt this way, you too may have felt something similar. I know that it's the only way to illustrate my inner world and an inner world that I'm certain other young girls are experiencing too.

These are some of the questions I was asking after the age of 9:

"What will they think of me?"

"Did I do something wrong?"

"Who should I be?"

"Why don't they like me?"

"What do they want from me?"

"How can I keep them all happy?"

"Why is this so hard?"

"Can I do anything right?"

"Why am I a failure?"

"Why don't things work out for me?"

Quite honestly, while my memory isn't the greatest, it's not hard to recall the way that I put myself down back then because, every once in a while, I start talking to myself like this again. The only difference is that now, when I catch myself being unkind, I know that I can choose new words and speak more kindly to myself.

MY WORDS CREATE MY WORLD

"My words create my world." This is a lesson that we teach all of the girls early on in our program. Why not give them a head start on things that so many women are only learning in their thirties and forties? If our language packs this much punch, let's get real about it, and let's start noticing some of the things we say (and hear) and how these words impact our daily lives. If our words create our truth, then why not use them to our advantage? Let's fast-forward to our lives today and ways that we might be using language that is still stunting our growth.

Here are some examples of how we block our own expansion (without even noticing!) by using words and language that keep us stuck and small.

I call this lack or self-limiting language:

- "These types of things only happen to me."
- "I will never be as successful as she is."
- "I'm worried about..."
- "I will try, but no promises."
- "I wasn't built that way."
- "There's never enough for me."
- "I wish I was more like..."

I want you to be brutally honest with yourself. Do you catch yourself saying some of these things? I know I still do… This chapter is for us.

STOP, DROP AND CHOOSE AGAIN

From now on, when you find yourself speaking in these self-defeating ways, I want you to take a moment to stop, drop the disempowering language and choose a new dialogue with yourself:

...something more empowering and uplifting

...something that makes you feel better on the inside

...something that you would be proud to say in front of an impressionable young girl

Here are some reframes to get you started:

- "I'm going to do everything I can to make this work and let go of the rest."
- "I get to define success on my own terms."
- "I am constantly inspired by the women around me."
- "There's always a way when I'm willing to think outside of the box."
- "There's always an opportunity to rock what I've got."
- "I'm always up for learning something new!"

Don't these sentences just *feel* softer and kinder? Try them on for size and see what works for you! The reframe is real, guys—I promise you that when you really start to notice your words and get intentional with them, you will start transforming and growing in ways you never thought would be possible from making such a small shift. I've literally seen it in action in my own life and in the lives of the women and girls I work with.

OUR INTERNAL DIALOGUE

I couldn't end this chapter without also talking about how important our inner conversations with ourselves are. Do you speak to yourself the way you would speak to someone you love? Most of us don't. We reserve all of our kindness and compassion for the other people in our lives and completely miss out on how important it is for us to be gentle and kind with ourselves. There is an inner radio station playing in our minds on the regular, dictating our experiences. Have you noticed it? It is literally laying out the spoken soundtrack of your life. It's narrating what's happening and your perception of it all. So I invite you to get well-acquainted with that voice and notice what it's saying on a moment-to-moment basis.

Ask yourself:

Is it a friendly voice?

Is it speaking in a kind way?

Does it speak words of empowerment and affirmation, or does it speak words that keep you stuck and small?

Is the voice a fountain or a drain?

If you start to notice that your inner voice is playing a role in your own disempowerment, change it up. As with all things, you get to choose what enters your consciousness. Imagine how you would feel moving through your life if the voice that speaks to you on the regular were supportive, friendly and loving.

SHE'S HEARING YOU

One of the most unfortunate things that I have witnessed is when women use harmful and downright mean language when they are describing themselves. Yes, I am 100% guilty of this myself. Our children look to us to set an example of self-worth. They follow our lead on the kind of relationship they have with themselves. When a valued female in a girl's life looks in the mirror and says something like, "I'm so fat" or "I look so awful," the child is going to naturally apply that language and perspective to herself. Instead, we can model a positive self-image by speaking of ourselves in a more gentle tone. I've said it before and I'll say it again, the work we do day in and day out in our relationship with ourselves will be the gift we give our girls. Improve the quality of your rapport and inner dialogue with yourself and you will change the way she feels about herself. It's a win/win really, and will reward us all with a new generation of more confident, self-aware and REAL girls.

STOP SHOULD-ING ON YOURSELF (AND ON OUR GIRLS)

On the topic of bad words, have you ever realized how powerless you feel when you use the word "should" in a sentence?... No seriously, think about it.

Personally, any information followed by the words "I should" is a huge indicator that I am carrying out something that someone else thinks I ought to do and adopting that idea as my own.

The next time you find that you are "shoulding" on

yourself, follow these steps to stop the disempowering language:

- Ask yourself if this is something that you are actively choosing to do or something that you feel is being imposed on you by a force outside of yourself (mom, friend, society, etc.).

- If you learn that you are doing what someone else is expecting of you and not what you want or feel is best for yourself, challenge the thought and make a conscious decision that is in line with YOUR personal values.

- If you learn that the words following "I should" are actually something that you do want, change up your language so that it reflects your active participation in the idea. A more empowering choice would be to say: "I choose/I could/I will..." Feeling forced is never a comforting feeling, and how we choose to perceive our ideas and thoughts is key!

POWER MANTRA STATION

On the topic of words and the effect they have on us, I want to share some power mantras that I like to use in my daily self-talk rituals. A belief is a thought you keep thinking and the words you keep speaking, so if you're serious about transforming your belief systems, you can start choosing new word structures to hit play on for the internal soundtrack of your life.

- I know that every moment is rigged in my favor.
- Everything I need is already inside of me.
- I am my own permission slip.
- I surround myself with people who uplift me.
- I am a source of light and love.
- I trust in the woman I am becoming.
- It is safe to let go of past versions of myself. I am evolving in every moment.
- I honor and release past versions of myself with love.
- I am responsible for the world I see. I get to choose my perspectives.
- In every moment, I get to choose who I am and who I want to be.
- I am powerful beyond measure.
- I am the creator of my own reality.
- I am evolving every minute of every day.
- I'm the kind of woman who gets everything she wants.

These are some of mine. I invite you to create your own.

Choose a power mantra and put it on your phone screen or on a sticky note on your mirror. These are such powerful reminders of your goal to be the leader in your own life and model that for our next generation.

I hope this chapter has helped you get honest about the way you communicate with yourself. If you've really taken this in, I can promise you that from here on out, you will start noticing your old language patterns in everyday conversations with yourself and with others. Now that you have the knowledge and the willingness you need to change it up, you can start using your words to reflect the reality that you actually want to create.

Today's heart-work is designed for you to get crystal clear about phrases and words that you're ready to part with so that when they show up for you, you can send them away and create new, more empowering language to use instead.

HEART ❤ WORK

Below, share some of the disempowering phrases that you're ready to drop once and for all!. Once you've written them out, I want you to literally put a big X over them and write down new, more empowering sentences that you want to replace the old ones with.

REFLECTIONS

REFLECTIONS

CHAPTER 7
THERE'S ALWAYS A CHOICE

"You always have a choice. Remember this when you start feeling like you don't have control over the circumstances of your life."

I feel like in order to truly step into our power and share that power, it's worth taking a moment to acknowledge where we've been and how that's shaped us… up until now. Why do I say "up until now"? Because we get to choose what's next. We get this big, beautiful, bold opportunity to look within, reflect and change what no longer serves us. We get to decide what we're available for and clear out the old thought patterns that are holding us back.

We are taught what we are taught as young girls, but as grown women, we get to choose what we keep and what we release. That's the part that's on us because when we know better, we can do better. Blaming our parents, teachers, political parties, etc. for our current states will totally keep us from being the women of our own dreams. Taking responsibility for who we choose to be in the here and now is what's important. When I'm ready to release old thought patterns handed down to me that make me feel disempowered, I imagine myself saying to the well-meaning adults who shaped my views: "Thanks for everything, but I'll take it from here." That's my way of drawing a line in the sand and declining old ways of thinking that make me feel stuck and small. I affirm that I get to choose a new way for myself.

THE POWER OF CHOICE

A big piece of understanding our own power is in acknowledging that we have the power of choice in most situations in life.

We get to choose:

- what we think
- what we say
- who our friends are
- how we behave
- what we eat
- how we spend our time
- how we love
- who we love
- what our spiritual practice is

The list goes on...

So often we look at the circumstances of our lives and determine that "Life is happening to me and I've got no say in how things play out." We unknowingly take a victim mentality and decide that we have zero control in our life circumstances, so we give up and give in. I want you to start playing your life full out and start acknowledging that life is actually happening for you as a result of your choices, your actions and your intentions.

CHOOSE TO STOP PLAYING THE BLAME GAME

I still do this. I hate to admit it, but I do. Being a powerful woman means that, in every moment, we take responsibility for our choices. We choose to be active rather than passive participants in our lives. We don't blame outside factors for who we are and what's happening in our life. Yes, a lot of crazy things can happen in life, but how we respond… well, that part is completely up to us.

When we blame a person, thing or circumstance for the way things are going in OUR life, we are basically declaring our powerlessness over our current state. In essence, we're giving up our power and relying on that same outside person, thing or circumstance to change things up for us to feel right. Is that realistic? We know that it's not because we cannot influence another person's actions in the same way that we can influence our own actions. Doesn't it just feel more empowering to look at where we can take responsibility for what's up and rely on our personal power to try and move things in the direction of our choosing? I hope your answer is a solid yes… and if it's not, I urge you to read the last paragraph again and again if necessary.

Nobody is coming to make your life the masterpiece that it can be. That is your job. Each of us is the lead character in the story of our own life and we need to act accordingly.

A question I often ask myself during the tough stuff is, "How would the most empowered version of me respond to this situation?" This helps me to pause and choose in a way that serves my highest good and accesses the most powerful version of me.

What area of your life will you start accepting more responsibility for?

CHOOSE YOUR OWN ADVENTURE

Who remembers these books from when they were a kid?

I may be aging myself here (lol) but, "Choose Your Own Adventure" books were my absolute favorite books to read when I was growing up because they put me in the driver's seat of the main character's life and, as a kid, I really loooooved that! These books give the reader the opportunity to choose from a variety of options that could play out in the story. I thought it was so powerful to see the domino effect of each choice that the main hero or heroine would make and their subsequent outcomes. I always enjoyed going back and choosing a different adventure to see how the characters' lives would have been altered if they had made a different decision when faced with a fork in the road. How does this apply to your life? How can you play a bigger role in creating your life by design? I'm giving you the keys to the kingdom here by reminding you to take the lead in your own life by making choices that reflect the woman you want to be. That's the woman who will lead our girls with courage, confidence and a profound knowing of who she truly is.

What adventure will you choose next for yourself?

KEEP YOUR PROMISES TO YOURSELF

Stop playing the waiting game. Start moving and shaking. So many people say that they want to live a certain kind of life, but they don't take the necessary action to make it a reality. Then they wonder why they're not where they want to be. We can choose to pave our way to a life that we love. It's great to set goals and intentions, but unless we take aligned action to reach those goals, we aren't going to create more of what we want in our lives. If we want to take the lead for our next generation, we've got to make moves and show them how it's done. It's imperative to make agreements with yourself and hold yourself to them. I have been wanting to write this book for three years, but somehow it never happened. I had the intention, but I wasn't taking any of the required steps to make this book a living, breathing thing. To get it going, I had to literally put myself on the hook by carving out designated writing time every week. I gathered together an amazing street team to share the book, and I got myself an editor. The book was in my heart, but it surely wasn't going to write itself. Once I had the necessary parameters and rituals in place, the circumstances were optimal for me to write my heart out. And from there, I was able to keep my promise to myself and birth this book.

What promises have you made to yourself that you will choose to keep?

BE MINDFUL OF THE PEOPLE YOU SURROUND YOURSELF WITH

Did you know that you start taking on the thoughts, beliefs, and characteristics of the five people you hang out with the most? They literally become the key influencers in our lives. Think about it… who are the five people you make the most time for, and are they people you would like to emulate? It's important to start taking notice of what character traits each member of your circle brings out in you. It's important to notice the kind of conversations you are having. Choose to be with the people who challenge you to be your best self and grow without putting you down when you fall off course. Surround yourself with the kind of women who want to shout out your victories to everyone they know because they feel your wins so deeply. You can't surround yourself with negative people and wonder why you're feeling stuck and uninspired. Find a community that supports your dreams and encourages you to think bigger and brighter. Then prepare for some serious growth. Remember this: At the top of that influencer list is YOU. So be sure to exemplify that quality relationship with yourself that you so deeply wish to create with those around you. As with all things, a positive relationship starts with you. Start treating yourself with the respect and kindness you deserve, and you will never settle for anything less in any of the friendships and relationships that you create throughout your life.

What kinds of friendships are you ready to release?

ACTIVELY CHOOSE YOUR PERCEPTIONS

If there is one thing I do as a coach with my clients, it is this: I help them to choose perspectives that serve them in their lives. There are so many different ways of looking at any given scenario, and when you choose to change the way you see things, your focus and your feelings can shift. Imagine this scenario: I am at a party, and a woman who is an acquaintance of mine walks by me a few times without saying hello, even after I try to catch her gaze and give her a smile. I finally decide that if she's not going to acknowledge that we know each other, I will. Why not, right? So I say my hello, and she gives me a cold hello back. My immediate next thought is this:

"What's her deal? Did I do something to offend her? What should I have done differently?"

In this example, I actively choose to get my back up and feel totally defensive about her response to me. This results in me feeling powerless, uncomfortable and slighted.

But what if I tried a different perception on for size? What if my internal response to her behavior was:

"She must be having a really tough day" or "She must be so in her head about something that she didn't even see or hear me."

In this example, I feel more in control and relaxed about the whole thing.

In the first example, I chose a perspective that

made it all about me. In the second one, I gave her the benefit of the doubt and didn't assume any responsibility for the way things played out.

This is a very small example of how a subtle shift in my perception; the way I chose to look at our exchange, could elicit two totally different feelings for me. It's important to choose the perceptions that keep you connected to your personal power. This was mine. Ultimately whatever her reason was for looking past me isn't what's important here. What is more relevant is the way that I choose to think about it and the amount of energy I choose to give it in my day.

How can you start choosing more empowering perspectives in your life?

CHOOSE AGAIN

There are always learning moments on the path to becoming the most elevated version of yourself. And while they might feel like a total bummer when we're experiencing them, they're worth their weight in gold when we're willing to use them to our advantage. I had a tough mom moment yesterday. I acted out of character. I lost my cool. I didn't use my tools. You will always hear me saying that my daughters are my greatest teachers, and yesterday was most definitely a testament to that. When my buttons were pushed, I chose to react in anger rather than respond with compassion. I chose to blame rather than look at my part of the interaction. Am I going to let this define my whole essence as a woman or a mother? Just a few years ago, I may have, but the answer from the woman I am today? HECK NO! Instead, I am going to make sure to talk to my daughter and take ownership of my part of the interaction that went sideways. I'm going to admit that I gave my power away and show her that I'm willing to own my mistakes. You see, when our girls see us as imperfect beings who sometimes falter, we are setting an example that is real and achievable. It's not about being perfect all of the time (or ever, really). It's about being a true woman, one who in every weak moment gives herself the grace to choose again. A woman who chooses a new perspective, a new response, a new behavior. We cannot define ourselves by the moments where we fall off course. We must instead applaud ourselves for the moments where we choose accountability and recommit to the women we want to be. The important thing to remember at times like this is that peace and empowerment are just a thought away. When I was able to lock into this idea, I gave myself the opportunity to choose a new thought and choose a new way of showing up for myself and my daughter. We always have the opportunity to choose again. I will say this again and again. There's so much beauty and grace in that.

In what areas of your life are you willing to make new, more empowered choices?

HEART ❤ WORK

Answer the prompt question at the end of each section in this chapter.

REFLECTIONS

REFLECTIONS

CHAPTER 8
ROCK YOUR RESILIENCY MUSCLES

We have all been gifted with superpowers: some that we were born with, and others that we have acquired through some of the challenging experiences in our lives."

You have superpowers… a lot of them!

Did you know this when you were growing up? I most definitely did not! In fact, when I was being raised, my elders would have thought that sharing messages like this one would result in kids who were "too full of themselves" or conceited in some way. My rebuttal to that is, if we aren't full of ourselves, then what are we full of?! As women, we have found praise in people telling us we are selfless. I want you to think about the true meaning of this for more than a moment. There is no virtue in being self-LESS—quite literally being without ourselves to be seen as virtuous. We may not notice these disempowering messages, but once we become aware of them, it's up to us to dismantle them for good. I often recall the way my late maternal grandmother thought of herself and others when they took a little bit of extra time with and for themselves. She had been taught that self-care was overindulgent and that, as a woman, if she wasn't doing for others all of the time, there was something wrong with her. As a child in observation mode, I could sense her feelings of guilt and discomfort if she perceived herself to be enjoying something too much. Oh, how I wished she were taught that being generous toward herself was a good thing and that experiencing joy wasn't something to be ashamed of. She passed this trait on to my mother—my mom accepted the baton and adopted these characteristics as her own. It's the natural thing to do after all, to embody the traits of your mother. But as time passed and my mom started to explore the old messaging she grew up with, she began to understand that she needed to change her narrative and that not caring for herself didn't serve her. I'm so grateful that she did that inner work to change that generational narrative so that my sisters and I could learn to be kinder and gentler with ourselves too. You see, with every new generation, we get to heal old patterns that no longer apply.

It is my deep desire to leave ideologies like this one behind for the highest good of ALL women and girls. When girls are introduced to their superpowers from a seed level, they will grow up with a limitless foundation: one that allows them to thrive through the good stuff and grow throughout the hard stuff… all while being in full possession of themselves. Can we create a new word and call it self-FULL? Can we teach kids to start noticing, acknowledging and rocking their superpowers? I know we can.

REALITY CHECK

While scrolling through social media, we might start believing that other women's personal and professional lives are always on the up and up. I think somewhere deep inside, we all know that that's simply not true and if we think it is, we've got our blinders on. Life is not a straight line. It will have us zigging and zagging all over the place, experiencing epic highs and extreme lows, and yet, however painful it all might seem, it's all working FOR us. Every experience is an opportunity to lean into our personal power and trust that we can grow from what life is presenting us with. Believe me, I didn't always feel this way. I used to take the hand I was dealt at times, kicking and screaming. It wasn't until I brought acceptance into the equation that I was able to move through the muck and actually experience the immense amount of light through the tunnel. It sounds cliche, but it's so damn true. True healing doesn't happen overnight, but one day into the future, you find yourself looking back and noticing that without that insane mountain you had to climb, you wouldn't have been granted the unshakable strength you have today. All that pain is actually where the light comes through, if only we are willing to let it in and rise with it.

STOP HIDING FROM THE PAIN

So many of us move through the world in an effort to literally avoid pain. We hide from it at all costs in hopes that it will never find us. It's inevitable though, isn't it? As part of the human family, we will experience varying degrees of pain and it will totally suck, and yet, it will all be worth it. Your pain will be uniquely designed for you. Literally hand-picked to bring you your very own brand of evolution. You see, your pain is your greatest teacher. Sounds out there, I know, but the sooner we can adopt this way of thinking, the more learning we can extract from the difficult times. Ultimately, each step in the pain game is giving us the greatest gift of all—the gift of resilience. What could be better than this? What could be better than knowing that through every uphill battle, you will come out stronger and more equipped for perseverance and success? More inner tools and inner resources set you up for a lifetime of personal power. Rock bottom will teach you lessons that mountain tops never will. I can promise you that.

YOUR PAIN REVEALS YOUR SUPERPOWERS

Once you've been nudged by the pain and found your own unique path through it, allow it to fuel and lift you. The thing about strength is that once you've located it within yourself, you have a really strong power source to guide you through future situations. When presented with another setback or pain point, you can rise to the challenge knowing that you've pulled through before and you will indeed pull through again. That's the true power of resiliency. Picture an elastic band that gets pulled in different directions and still comes back. Us humans? When we get stretched out and knocked down, we can come back even stronger. You can have that same immediate comeback rate as your inner toolkit starts getting more and more accessible to you.

There was a very, very tough time in my life when

mine and my husband's dream of becoming parents seemed nearly impossible. Doctors and specialists told us that it would never happen and that we should pursue other options. It was one of the most heart-shattering experiences of our lives to hear those words. With every failed IVF cycle, the doctors' feedback became less promising. Each day that passed, when we thought we couldn't take another heartbreak, we somehow found the strength to push through and keep moving in the direction of our dream. Ultimately, many medical procedures and IVF cycles into our fertility journey, we were blessed with twin daughters who, as I write this book, are 15 years old. The lesson here isn't that we were finally able to grow our family (that was the bonus). The true learning that came from all the pain is that by finding a way through it, I released an older version of myself who no longer served me. I released a woman who, once upon a time, let the world tell her who she was—a woman who wouldn't go after her dreams because they seemed too big or out of reach. This very long and painful experience birthed the woman I am today—a woman who believes in her own power and works every day to introduce others to theirs. One of my greatest accomplishments to date, the creation of my business and movement as a whole, came from my journey through the pain into my path of radical resilience. You see, as soon as I was really able to experience the life-changing magic of resilience through this very painful life event, I wanted to share it with every woman and young girl that I knew. I wanted to scream it off the rooftops and that's exactly what I did. Our entire curriculum is designed to teach girls about all the different tools that live inside of them. Tools that can be used to guide them through every life experience with ease and grace. I didn't want another girl or woman to experience a challenge without knowing they have an inner guidance system to help them move AND grow through it.

TURNING PAIN INTO PURPOSE

One of my favorite Rumi quotes, "Live life as if everything is rigged in your favor," has become my daily morning mantra. As I started to heal from the experiences that were on my own path, I started to feel stronger and more motivated to give a greater meaning to the pain. I wanted to somehow serve others with all the new growth that had been presented to me through all of my personal ups and downs and rites of passage. I felt that if I could redefine my pain, then I could give purpose to all the shit I had to go through... and so I got to work. When my girls were less than a year old, I went back to school and became a certified empowerment coach—a role that would literally change the course of my life. That role gave way to the creation of GiRLiFE. When I look at the impact that our movement has had and the number of girls whose lives we have been able to touch through our work, I can never look back with regret, with pain or with a "why me?" perspective. I can only look back and know that it was all working out for the highest good of all. It was rigged in my favor, and that knowledge gives me a completely different way of looking at an otherwise harrowing experience. That knowledge gives me peace. This is the perspective that I choose for myself every single day. This is the perspective that gives me strength, and whenever the sad memories start coming over me again, I declare for myself: "I choose peace instead of this." Pain? It's inevitable. But suffering?

Well…that's optional.

WHAT DOES THIS MEAN FOR OUR GIRLS?

Now I'm not saying that our girls should see us on a constant emotional roller coaster or that we should put everything out there for them to internalize. I am, however, suggesting that we give them the opportunity to witness us moving through some of our own hardships so that they can reflect that back in their own lives. For some women, it can feel instinctual to want to shield girls from the challenges of the outside world and pretend that everything is "perfect" all the time. I know that as a parent, I still do this at times without even noticing it. I try to hush my husband if we're having a conflict in front of our daughters or shield my girls from the day's heartbreaking news report. The problem with this is that we're giving our girls the wrong message. If they view our inner and outer lives as perfect all the time, what will happen when a problem arises (and a problem will arise)? It will hit them HARD, because they never witnessed the people closest to them working through their own stuff. We owe it to our girls to be real with them. To show them that while challenges will exist, and while they will inevitably experience pain, they will always find a way through. I always invite our facilitators to share their own resiliency stories with the girls in their workshops so that our girls can witness firsthand how one woman has grown from some of the tough stuff that was happening for her. It gives them the firsthand example they need to understand that they too can persevere, even when roadblocks appear, as they inevitably do. Let's not delay our girls' growth any further by robbing them from their inevitable pain and rites of passage. Instead, let's show them how we've come out on the other side and that we've done it with grace. We've felt the feelings, released the pain and turned our experiences into power. That's what our girls need right now. To know that they've got some serious resiliency muscles that will unveil an unshakeable strength when given the opportunity.

HEART ♥ WORK

The next time you find yourself in a challenge, ask yourself these questions:

Where is the lesson?

How is this experience my greatest teacher?

How is this working for me?

How can I choose to be more real for the girls in my life?

REFLECTIONS

REFLECTIONS

CHAPTER 9
STOP GHOSTING YOUR DREAMS

"There are people out there who are way less talented and/or qualified than you, living out their dreams because they decided to say yes to themselves. Stop ghosting your dreams."

Have you ever watched a little baby trying to figure out how to walk? They literally fall down dozens of times in one exploration session, and it never even crosses their mind to stop trying. Not even for a second does it occur to them that they won't eventually get up because intuitively, somehow, they know that they will. And they will continue stumbling, pushing, falling and falling until they are walking, running and then eventually sprinting. I believe that their success comes from their confidence. They're not judging themselves or feeling judged. They're literally just doing what feels right in the moment and what feels right is to keep trucking along. That baby is so present in that moment that nothing is going to take him/her off course. Talk about an unstoppable mindset. That's where the magic happens.

So what is it that happens to us as we get older that stops us from going after what we so badly want? Why do we believe that a couple of failures should stop us from continuing to try? It's different for all of us, but as a young girl, I can definitely recall moments in the classroom or with well-meaning adults when I was scolded for not getting something right the first time. I also remember being scolded for doing something in a way that was different from "the way" that had been laid out. I didn't always feel encouraged to try because failure was frowned upon. It was as simple as that. So somewhere in my psyche, I created this rule that I would never try something new unless I was one hundred percent sure that it would be successful. And let's be honest… What were the chances of that? So basically, I was rarely willing to try anything new, and I dismissed every desire that was ever on my heart for fear that I wouldn't get it right the first time around. Sad, huh? I know I wasn't alone in this. So many of the women I coach had created the same unspoken internal understanding that unless the conditions were optimal, they would not be moving on any new ideas.

YOU KNOW/ARE THE ANSWER

The odds of you being born are about 1 in 400 trillion. Let that sink in for a moment. You are the answer to someone's prayers. You have a valuable gift to give. You have a brilliant voice to share. You being the highest expression of your own truth is needed on our planet. You are here for a reason. I believe you already may know what that reason is somewhere within you. Your intuition may have revealed it to you at different times, and you may have pushed back and denied yourself the opportunity to truly explore it. Perhaps now is your time. Perhaps, this chapter is for you. You're a one-time magical masterpiece. You, simply being you is a once-in-forever miracle. Never underestimate the importance of your presence. You matter. Please act accordingly.

THE ART OF FAILING FORWARD

One of the workshops we offer to young girls is called "The Leader in Me." In this workshop, we teach girls that one very important characteristic of a true leader is that they are willing to fail. When I taught this lesson to the girls in our workshops, they were in shock. They challenged me in every possible way, certain that being a leader could never be associated with failure. I really had to challenge their thinking and give them examples of so many brilliant creators and thought leaders who failed multiple times before they succeeded in introducing their unique craft to the world. JK Rowling, Thomas Edison, Oprah Winfrey, Michael Jordan… the list goes on. While changing their perception on this was really hard, the rewards were well worth it. Imagine how many future gifts these young girls may bestow on our planet by simply getting back on the horse when an idea has a different outcome than the one they anticipated the first time around. Imagine how much education and information they will receive with each failed attempt. I get goosebumps just thinking about how this reframe can change things up for us and for our girls. Sara Blakely, the creator of Spanx, recalls how every night at the dinner table, her father would ask, "How did you fail today?" He actually encouraged his children to fail in some way, each and every day, and if they didn't have a failure report of the day for him, he would encourage them once more to go out there and find something to fail at. How amazing is that? His rationale was that if his kids were failing, then he had all the proof he needed that they were trying. And guess what? His daughter went on to become a world renowned inventor and entrepreneur. Was her creation a straight line? Heck no! She failed and failed creating prototype after prototype until she created Spanx. If that's not a testament to the gift of failure, I don't know what is.

SCREW PERFECT

The quest for perfection is a silent dream killer. We try so hard to make everything "perfect"—the conditions, our actions, our execution plan—that we never start. It's so exhausting to strive for excellence when we haven't even gotten our feet wet. You know what wins the game though? Imperfect action! It's never going to be perfect (because perfection doesn't exist), but by creating a plan and then bringing that plan to life, we're moving in the right direction. In the beginning of this book, I touched on my own creative and entrepreneurial journey, and I want to stress it here again. If I'd waited for the conditions to perfect before I started GiRLiFE, I'd still be working at a job that didn't move or inspire me. If I had not released my own relentless struggle with perfectionism, I never would have launched the thing. In this program, we teach female leaders how to run their own profitable girls' empowerment businesses. Was it everything I wanted it to be out of the gate? Absolutely not! It was a work in progress and, quite frankly, it still is. I have changed and updated the curriculum, our messaging and our platform at least ten times. You know what remained constant though? I always stayed committed to the evolution of the brand and of our offerings. I put in the heart-work day in and day out to learn and grow in my business. And on days when I fail, I give myself the grace to keep moving forward and try again. Having a clear intention and staying aligned with your dreams—that's what can get you out of the funk of perfection.

Every woman who joins us as a GiRLiFE Facilitator empowers herself and roughly 100 girls in her community. At the time that this book is being published, we have 170 facilitators. That's 170 women who are living out their dreams and 17,000 girls who are being taught to access their superpowers because I was willing to put aside my quest for perfection and step into imperfect action. I'm doing the math and sharing the stats to drive home the impact that would be missing in the world if I didn't step into my life's work. Multiply that by the billions of people in our world who don't act on the desires of their heart for fear of perfection and imagine what the world is being robbed of. Step into your light, beautiful soul. Don't wait for perfection. It doesn't exist. What does exist? You, with all of your gorgeous imperfections that actually make you the masterpiece that you are. Don't let your brilliant ideas just be ideas. Instead, believe in yourself and take inspired action.

DO WHAT FEELS GOOD WITHOUT QUESTIONING IT

My sister in Toronto recently sent me a video of

her three kids dancing. This is how I get the opportunity to watch and enjoy them growing up, since we're not in the same city. In this particular video, my two-year old niece was so in the zone. You know that phrase, "Dance like nobody's watching?" That was her. She was feeling the music and expressing her pure excitement for the moment. Every couple of seconds, she would turn to her mom and say, "FUN!" She was literally living her bliss in those moments. She wasn't questioning what people were thinking of her or how great of a dancer she is. She just was. We so often do things in life with so much self-analysis and critique that it takes away the joy of the activity itself. We don't move on passions or big ideas because we judge ourselves before we even take the first step. What if we approached the desires of our hearts like my two-year-old niece? What if we took on new opportunities with a sense of wonderment that got us focused on the process and not the outcome?

In my experience, it wasn't until I started taking more imperfect action that I started to evolve from that timid, fearful young girl into a more self-assured woman. I started getting more comfortable with doing things because they were fun or felt good, and less obsessed with the outcomes. Let me tell you, was this ever freeing! My goal in my work with women and girls is simple—I want us to bottle up that curiosity, self-belief and follow-through that we as children would never have thought twice about. I want us to live life on our own terms with the same confidence and determination of our younger, bolder selves.

BEWARE OF WHO YOU SHARE YOUR DREAMS WITH (AT FIRST)

On your journey to following your dreams, please don't look to people who never followed their dreams to support and lead you to where you're trying to go. Chances are that if you do, they will tell you to "be realistic" or tell you "it's impossible—if it were possible, it would have been done already." You will experience many naysayers telling you to stick to what you know and to not think outside the box. Their fear is contagious, and if you hang out with them long enough, they just might talk you out of moving on those goals. When I first had the idea for my girls' empowerment business, I was so fortunate to have so many people in my corner cheering me on and believing in my vision. I did, however, have an equal number of people telling me that my idea could never work and that nobody would pay money for girls' empowerment programming. Guess which of the two voices I decided to listen to? While I was tempted to give up before I even tried because of some of the less inspiring feedback I received, I had a deep, intense knowing that this could and would work, and that, with my business model, we would indeed touch the lives of thousands of girls across the globe. Every visionary I know was willing to take on a different way of thinking and trust their intuitive hits without needing others to buy into them too. I want this for you too. Turn up the volume on what YOU know to be your own truth so that you don't get sidetracked with unnecessary feedback. And stop asking other people for directions to places they've never actually been. How could they possibly be your guide if they've never actually done what you want to do?

PERMISSION TO COLOR OUTSIDE THE LINES

I distinctly remember being in kindergarten, sitting at my desk and coloring in my book. My teacher was looking over my shoulder, saying, "Melody, stop coloring outside the lines. Your drawing won't look right if you do!" Even as a young girl, those instructions felt wrong to me. I remember thinking, "What if coloring outside the lines would actually help me to create something more unique and different that you've never seen before?" Of course, I turned the volume down on that (brilliant) inner voice and continued "coloring inside the lines" as well as I could, and as I was instructed to do, until l I was well into my thirties. I'm reminded of this analogy so often in different areas of my life and I'm so glad I decided to finally break that mold and start creating my own rules for life and work. You see, we're not built to fit in boxes, we're built to fit out. If I had continued to "color inside the lines," I most definitely would not be doing what I'm doing today in my personal and professional life. I had to step out, write new rules that better applied to me and start moving on my own dreams. So this chapter right here is your green light to move on your dream, however messy or far out it might seem. Don't listen to that voice of fear that tells you you're not ready, or that it has to be done in a certain way, or that you should be realistic. Be your own permission slip and be willing to color outside the lines. Be willing to fit out and do it YOUR way. I dare you to be UNrealistic. You see, we're all so lit up by this idea of teaching girls to chase their dreams, meanwhile, we're ghosting our own dreams. That's just not how this works. We've got to be willing to get our hands dirty, to do the thing that we so deeply want them to do and lead by example. I don't care how old you are or how under or overqualified you think you are… go take action on the dream that's on your soul. Be the woman who feels scared and does it anyway because her desire for impact is greater than her fear. When we can give more energy to our dreams than we do to our fears, we can create opportunities in every corner of our lives.

Do it messy.

Do it scared.

Just do it.

Please.

HEART ♥ WORK

What have you failed at today?

What's one thing you've stopped yourself from doing because you were so focused on being the best at it, that you stopped before you even started?

How are you willing to start coloring outside the lines?

REFLECTIONS

REFLECTIONS

CHAPTER 10
ROCK YOUR KINDNESS

"Anything you want to do, be or create in this life, will be deepened exponentially when done with kindness."

As a reader of this book, I already know this about you—that you want to heal the planet for our next generation. I believe that showing kindness and compassion for ourselves and for those around us is the medicine that we have to give a world that is in desperate need of repair. We all have the intention of being kind but are often sidetracked by our busy schedules, our ever growing lists of to-do's and those tiny little devices that have the potential to take us down in every moment of the day… Yes, I'm talking about our phones. We all do it. I know I do it for sure. I sometimes look down at my phone more than I look up at the person I'm having dinner with. Sadly, that's me trying to make an effort to be present and still, it happens. So my offering in this chapter is to truly set an intention to stay present with yourself and those around you and rock your kindness in a way that only you can. Please note that as with all things, we need to master our own inner kindness game first. We must speak and act with kindness for ourselves first and then take it out into the world.

GRATITUDE

I know it deep within my bones that a gratitude practice is at the starting point of all kindness practices. When we can find reasons to feel thankful every day, even when things are tough, that is the purest form of self-kindness that there is. This is precisely how we fill our own cup before attempting to do so for others. That gratitude every day makes our ability to deliver kindness completely unconditional, which is what we are trying to create more of—unconditional love for ourselves and for others. Gratitude has the power to turn everything into enough, and when we have enough and know that we are enough, kindness and compassion can flow effortlessly. Do you have a gratitude practice? Our program's Gratitude Workshop is the very first workshop I ever created because I wanted girls to know that within them lies one of the greatest, most impactful tools that they have available to them. This is one of our most successful workshops to date for that very reason. We have this unique opportunity to pay this knowledge forward to our girls! If you don't already have one, consider adopting a daily gratitude practice. I like to set some time aside at the very end of every evening to list out at least ten items that I am grateful for. At the top of my list is always my family and friends and my deep gratitude for being able to do work that I love every single day. My first thought and prayer every morning is, "thank you – what a blessing it is to be granted another day on this earth."

WE RISE BY LIFTING OTHERS

One of my favorite quotes is by Robert Ingersoll: "We rise by lifting others." I have practiced this in my own life and know it to be true. When we take a moment to step outside of ourselves with an open heart and a willingness to do or give to someone else, we are giving ourselves the greatest gift. It's an intoxicating feeling to give simply for the joy of giving, without expecting or wanting anything in return. I have often told my clients that when you are feeling down, find a way to lift someone else up, and they've all come back to me with the same feedback. Not only does it work, but the gratitude from the person on the receiving end literally raises them up. Each of us has been given our own unique ways of lifting others up. You could give your time, your talent, your money, your kind acts. I will never forget the day my husband and my daughter went to a hospital in the city to sing and play guitar for children who were being treated for various conditions. My daughter came home that day lit up that she was able to bring a little bit of sunshine into the life of someone who was struggling. She shared that one of the kid's mothers was sobbing tears of joy and gratitude for the gift of their time and the music that they had given her daughter. A simple gesture that seems small to you can make all the difference in someone else's life.

DO IT WITH KINDNESS

Every outcome that you ever want to achieve can be better achieved with kindness. You may be rolling your eyes right now, but I'm being totally serious! This has been my experience, and I had the best role models who demonstrated this for me as I was growing up. When I was a young girl, my parents were experiencing a lot of challenges as immigrants in a new country trying to acclimate to the language, the culture, the people, etc., and still every exchange was met with kindness. I feel grateful to have learned early on that kindness is magic. It opens the door to true human connection. And when we treat others with love and kindness, it becomes more natural to treat ourselves this way too. Kindness is easier when things are going well, but when challenges arise and we lean into kindness, invisible doors can open for us—doors that anger and hate could never open.

HAVE MORE COMPASSION

Do you know what's going on in someone else's life? I mean really, really know? I'm willing to bet that you don't. So many of us hide some of the really difficult stuff we're going through because we fear the stigma of being seen in a certain way, or because we want to keep our private lives private. So let's just say it's safe to assume that most people are dealing with their own set of inner battles, no matter how much they smile, laugh and make us believe that everything is "perfect." Now imagine that every single human on this planet decided to show up with a little more compassion every single day. Can you imagine the ripple effect that would have on our consciousness as a whole? What does it mean to show up with more compassion? It can be as simple as having eye contact with someone as they share something with us and asking them follow-up questions to let them know they've been seen and heard. Your unique brand of compassion is exactly what the world needs more of.

BRING THE SUNSHINE

I'm the first to say that we can't change another person, but I can promise you this: when you show up as your highest, most authentic self, people can't help but take notice. While they may not know it on a conscious level, I can promise you that they will feel it on a subconscious level. It's an energetic exchange, and by making an effort to bring your sunshine, everybody wins. It's contagious. Smiles are contagious. Laughter is contagious. Kindness is contagious. So why not start spreading more of a good thing? What a special opportunity we have as women to model a way of operating in the world that is filled with compassion. I can promise you this: kind women will go farther. They will be the recipients of more success, more fulfillment and more inner peace. Are you with me in walking our talk for our girls? I know you are. Let's bring the sunshine!

RANDOM ACTS OF KINDNESS

We each have this unique ability to do simple random acts of kindness all day long. They're not difficult to do, and they're easily accessible to all. Have you ever been the recipient of a random act of kindness by a stranger? I have, and I will tell you that it's not only the warmest feeling ever, but it also fills you with a deep desire to pay it forward and do something similar for another stranger.

Here are some ideas to get you started:

- Buy coffee for the person behind you at your favorite drive-thru.
- Leave a kind note in someone's mailbox.
- Create kindness rocks and distribute them in your community.
- Send an email to someone who you admire
- Give an unexpected compliment.
- Leave a review for someone's podcast, restaurant, book, etc.
- Send a handwritten thank-you note to someone who has impacted you.
- Put a quarter in someone's expired parking meter.

HEART ♥ WORK

What is your gratitude practice?

Can you commit to two random acts of kindness this week?

REFLECTIONS

REFLECTIONS

CHAPTER 11
IMPERFECT WOMEN MAKE PERFECT ROLE MODELS

"How many dreams never moved their way up from the backburner because you're still waiting for perfection? How many experiences did you block from your life while you waited for the perfect circumstances? How many outfits sit in your closet with the tags still hanging off of them as you wait for that perfect occasion?"

As women, we have been caught up in a highly dysfunctional cycle of "perfectionism," and, quite frankly, not only am I tired of it, but I will continue to speak on it as often as I can in the content I share. I want to demystify this idea that we need to be the absolute best in everything that we do, at all costs. Somewhere along the way, we started to believe that perfectionism is a virtue: something to strive towards and embody. We believed the lie that we had to be perfect in every role that we play: mother, sister, daughter, friend, business woman, mentor… you fill in the blank. I know you know what I'm talking about.

And you know what the most important piece in all

of this is? That we break this cycle of perfection-seeking because our girls are taking notes. They are following every example of this that we set for them. If we continue to model striving for perfection, they too will set standards for themselves that are unattainable. They too will get caught in a web of disappointment every time they fall short of perfect. Why do that to them? Why do that to us?

As a young girl, I thought of myself as a serial quitter. I would start something, take a few lessons, let the disappointment set in that I wasn't the best (and I most definitely wasn't "perfect" at the thing), and give it up. Piano, gymnastics, dance, volleyball, you name it. It was most definitely ingrained somewhere in my belief system that being perfect was something to reach for, and every time I fell short of perfect, (which was only ALL the time because it does NOT exist), I was angry with myself. I was putting a condition on my self-love and that is dangerous territory to live in. That was grounds for a poor relationship with myself that would surely play out later on in my life. Spoiler alert: it totally did.

Here are a few reframes I would like to offer to little Melody and perhaps to the young girl within you who probably needs to hear this new messaging:

IT DOESN'T NEED TO BE PERFECT TO BE GOOD

You were experimenting, learning and growing. You were figuring out what you enjoy, what feels right, and what it is that gets you excited about living. If we make girls feel like they're quitting while they're trying on new hobbies, ideas, and identities for size, then we are robbing them of learning so much about themselves. The truth is nobody can do everything forever. So why make them feel bad about the research phase of life? It's important to understand that we are evolving beings. Change is our birthright. So let's not hold our girls (or ourselves) to everything they set their sights on. Let's create an environment where they can change their minds and try new things. This doesn't mean that they should dabble in every single thing they ever do, but it does mean that if they've tried something and given it a fair chance, they can have the freedom to move on from it without feeling like they've done something wrong.

YOU DON'T HAVE TO BE GREAT AT SOMETHING YOU LOVE TO DO

It's okay to enjoy an activity and not be great at it. Please read that again. During our short time here on earth, wouldn't it be nice to grant ourselves the opportunity to do the things we love to do without being attached to this idea that we must be the best or even good at them? Here's an example: I am not the BEST singer. I may not even be a good singer, but I really enjoy singing. So should I stop myself from singing when I'm feeling moved by the music? Should I rob myself of the joy that I experience when I'm belting out my tunes? Uh-uh! No! Now I'm not saying I'm going to get on a stage and sing for other people, but if it's lighting me up, why can't I sing in the shower or throughout my day for myself? Isn't life meant to be enjoyed? Can you think of an example of this in your own life? Let's start normalizing doing things simply for the joy of doing them and not because we have to be the best.

KEEP GOING

Imagine with me for a second. I want you to think of one of your favorite artists, musicians, or writers. Hold for a moment in your mind's eye, a creation of theirs that has totally moved and inspired you. Perhaps it's a song, a movie or a book. Think of how their masterpiece makes you feel. Now ask yourself what it would be like if this creation had never existed?... Think about all the art and brilliance that would be lacking in our world. For every idea, product, or entity that has ever come into existence, there has also been a visionary who was willing to be messy and imperfect. Their willingness to try the thing, fail at the thing, and keep evolving the thing, is what gifted us with their offering that is now being enjoyed by the entire world. Seriously though, could you imagine a world where the song "Sir Duke" didn't exist because Steve Wonder didn't think it was "perfect" enough to release? What about the show Friends that's been viewed and loved by billions of people around the world? What if Marta Kauffman decided that because the storyline or characters weren't "perfect" enough, she wouldn't ever release the show? What if Maya Angelou never released her stunning poetry to the world because she was paralyzed by the fear of making every piece "perfect"? We would be missing out on so much raw talent if this was the case for every human who ever had a creative idea but decided to keep to themselves because they were plagued by perfection paralysis.

YOU'VE GOT THE RIGHT STUFF

Every dream, hope, and wish that is implanted in

your heart is there for a reason. And everything you need to bring that into fruition is already inside of you. By this point in our time together, I know you know that the empowerment you so deeply crave for yourself is right there waiting to be uncovered. You've got what it takes. You've got the heart for it. You've got your very own unique set of gifts. The things you dream of doing are not arbitrary. They are showing up because they are yours to reveal, share, and teach, in all of your beauty and brilliance. So don't shy away from it because it's not wrapped up in a perfect bow. Move closer to it and be willing to explore it, messy. You have a one-of-a-kind imprint to leave on the world. Please don't take that lightly. If the dream is in you, it's most definitely for you.

HEART ♥ WORK

What project, dream for goal (however big or small it may be) are you willing to take messy action on right now?

What is the first step you need to take to move on that goal?

REFLECTIONS

REFLECTIONS

CONCLUSION
YOUR LEGACY AWAITS

"What a beautiful gift it is that when we discover a new way of operating in the world, we inspire others by simply being the highest expression of our own truth."

What part will you play in creating a legacy of generational female empowerment? At this point on our journey together, my hope is that you are fully committed to your own evolution, knowing that it will help you step into your highest self and that it may also be the catalyst to unlocking empowerment for our girls. They are a true reflection of us, revealing to us in every moment how we've grown.

LET'S REDEFINE NINE

Earlier on, I shared the chilling statistic that a girl's self-confidence peaks at nine years of age. Nine is the age that girls begin to hide who they are so that they can become who this world expects them to be (heartbreaking, I know). Hearing this was all I needed to kick my heart-centered business into high gear. It became my driving force to change things up for our next generation, and it continues to be on the heart of every facilitator out there bringing empowerment to their local girls. Our work as women is to pay it forward for our girls and find unique ways to give a new meaning to this tender young age. Together we can redefine nine as the age where girls rise up and shine in spite of the plans the world may have mapped out for them. We get to show girls a reality that inspires them to locate their inner power and know that it will serve them throughout their entire lives and in all circumstances. No more holding back. No more playing small. Only growing their power with each passing day.

How can you take your desire for serving the female leaders of tomorrow one step further? You already know the most significant way—walk your talk by modeling the characteristics that you want to nurture within them. What else? There are so many inspiring and impactful things you can do. Perhaps you will start mentoring a young girl in your life. Or maybe you will start your very own girls' empowerment or women's group in your community. You might choose to create a social media platform where you share what empowerment means to you. I want you to know that each idea will be given its wings only when you bring your unique gifts, experiences and perspectives to it. YOU are the secret formula, and when you truly own and embody that, oooooh, well, that's everything. How cool is it that you get to use your superpowers to empower others? The coolest.

Whatever you decide is your next level of empowerment, open your heart and lead with your light.

Your authentic truth is your birthright and the only thing that this world wants and needs from you—the only thing our girls need and want from you. You are sitting on gold. Every challenge, every victory, every inner tool you've chosen to lean into… these are the gifts you have to share. Stop waiting. Start sharing. We need you.

Throughout the pages of this book, you have been presented with many ways to give that empowerment you so deeply crave to yourself so that our next generation can thrive. The ball is in your court, beautiful reader. The rest is up to you. Nobody is going to hand you a permission slip to step into that next level of your evolution. Only you can do that. Only you can crown yourself as the visionary leader in your own life. When you choose yourself, you choose our girls. How beautiful a thing it is that when we break through our own glass ceiling, we get to watch our girls break through theirs? No more limited thinking. No more holding back. Rocking our imperfections every step of the way. Thank you for showing up for the important work we've done here together. YOU stepping up in this way will heal future generations of women. That is my promise to you.

It's been an honor to take this adventure with you and hold space for you as you navigate on your journey. Turn your light all the way up and rock your empowerment in a way that only you can. Take pride in the profound ripple effect you are igniting for our female visionaries of tomorrow. YOU are, you were and will always be powerful beyond measure.

XOXO,
Melody

ACKNOWLEDGMENTS

To my incredible parents, siblings, extended family and dear friends, thank you for your constant support and for embodying all that is love. Each of you is a brilliant light in my life.

To my incredible husband, thank you for your endless love and companionship. Most importantly, thank you for being a wise and listening ear for all of my GiRLiFE daydreams. I am grateful for our love.

To my daughters, Noa and Ella, your deep inner knowing of who you are continues to inspire me. Thank you for being my greatest teachers in this life. I love you.

To my beautiful GiRLiFE Facilitators, thank you for walking this path with me. You each inspire me every day with your courage and add fuel to our collective mission for girls empowerment.

To the incredible army of angels who have come together to bring this book to life, I am forever thankful. Big shout out to Marissa LaRocca, Stephanie Burns Robertozzi, Meg Brunson and Cara Alwill. I appreciate you all so much.

ABOUT THE AUTHOR

Melody Pourmoradi is on a mission to introduce women and girls alike to their many superpowers. She is an empowerment coach, author and host of The Empowering Her Podcast. As founder of The GiRLiFE Certification Program, she teaches women how to run impactful and profitable girls empowerment businesses. She is passionate about teaching women that their valuable work in the world deserves to be recognized and compensated. Her greatest goal is for every girl and woman to know that they are powerful beyond measure and that they can create a life that lights them up from the inside out. Melody is married to the love of her life, and together, they are proud parents of twin girls.

CONNECT WITH MELODY

Listen to the **Empowering Her Podcast** on your favorite podcast app.

Follow her on Instagram:
@GiRLiFEempowerment

Join her GiRLiFE Facebook Group:
www.facebook.com/groups/girlsempowermentbiz

Check out her Website:
www.getgirlpower.com

Read her first book:
XOXO, from a girl who gets it: Life Notes for the Young Girl Within

We have an empowerment gift to share with our community of readers.
It can be redeemed here:
melodypourmoradi.com/bookbonus

Please join our private Facebook group to connect with other empowered readers!
www.facebook.com/groups/empoweredwomenempowergirls

Made in the USA
Middletown, DE
27 August 2022

72371537R00097